Susie Wild is author of the short story collection *The Art of Contraception* (Parthian, 2010) listed for the Edge Hill Prize, and the novella *Arrivals* (Parthian, 2011). Her writing appears in publications like *Poetry Digest, The Lonely Crowd,* Wales Arts Review, *The Lampeter Review,* and *Rising.* She has an MA in Creative Writing from Swansea University and an MA in Journalism from Goldsmiths. Awarded a place on Ty Newydd's poetry masterclass, she has studied creative writing with Gillian Clarke and Imtiaz Dharker. She was writer in residence at the Mothership, Dorset, and her poems have been an Ink Sweat & Tears Pick of the Month, and a First Thursday performance winner. She has performed her poems at events like Glastonbury Festival, Hay Festival, Green Man Festival and the Dylan Weekend. Her recent multimedia commission, 'Sex Change Disco,' in collaboration with artist Beth Greenhalgh, was performed at Made in Roath and Cardiff Contemporary 2016. Born in London, she spent her childhood in Devon and Cornwall. She now lives in a house in Cardiff with a German prop maker and their Welsh cat.

Twitter: @Soozerama

Wildlife Blog: http://susiewild.blogspot.co.uk

T0098445

Better Houses

Susie Wild

Parthian, Cardigan SA43 1ED
www.parthianbooks.com
First published in 2017
© Susie Wild 2017
ISBN 978-1-912109-66-1
Editor: Zoë Brigley
Cover design by Torben Schacht
Typeset by Elaine Sharples
Printed in EU by Pulsio SARL
Published with the financial support of the Welsh Books Council British Library
Cataloguing in Publication Data
A cataloguing record for this book is available from the British Library.

For Torben, who makes everything better, including me

Contents

Build the Table First

I want everything to catch
fire but not actually

burn. I need breakable glasses
for each re-enacted fight
so I can know nothing
is broken between us

for long. I want flamingoes
in flight; a thought that looks like
broccoli, blood, so much

fake blood. Rush in, please, and try
to understand my nonsense,
the gaps
between what I need

and want. Sit through meetings, take
notes. Reinforce the furniture
against unskilled stagehands,
touring all our house moves.

A Beginner's Guide to Mourning

Bait with perfume
– jasmine, honeysuckle –
set up the light trap

at dusk. Start in your garden.

Close your
mouth. Whatever the season,
hope for steady drizzle.

Wait for a flit of them.

On waking, examine your haul,
see the many lace-winged insects
daring to visit their upside-down house.

There is no need to kill, but

you will anyway, sedating hawk-moths,
splendid brocades, dingy skippers,
in ammonia jars.

Pin specimens to paper

– pillows of feathered bark –
piercing thorax after thorax. Air
in the cupboard for a fortnight.

Frame the best for your
hallway, stilled, until all the lights
of the house are switched off.

Carcharodon Carcharias, Cariad

In the restaurant, feed
on crab cakes, flex the shells
of mussels, pour wine like Brody
when Hooper dives in for dinner: 'Are you going to eat that?'
your jaws wide.

Later, swig shark
   bites on the esplanade,
      in this *summer town of summer dollars*,
                    Penarth Pier port,
                        Ilfracoombe starboard,
                            the horizon swims
                        parallel to village bunting,
          inverted fins in Amity Beach
   yellow, vineyard red———

Watermelon squalus break the surface of a sea
of cocktails, cupped
in city hands. Down them clinically. Drink
to your legs. Fool around. On the roof terrace,

search for bigger boats. As the sun
dips and the tide turns, notice how Flat
Holm and Steep Holm still look like islands

from the shore. When the film starts, be a rogue hunk
of Quint – dangerous and dastardly – quoting the script

verbatim. When the credits roll and the sky has
eaten the light, be bowlegged women, be land-legged

on water. Like half-arsed astronauts, look beyond
the clouds for an outburst of meteors. Find none.

Keep kicking, full throttle.

Contemplate fishing. Ask sea dogs
to show you the way home.

Have one more drink.
        Up the ante.
            Cut everything open,
              spill
                  your—

                          guts.

The Lash Museum

A gusty Cornish wind
slammed the caravan shut,
skinning a birthmark,
my head
a blood fountain.

Holding my doll by a pigtail,
I stood at the swinging door,
my pinafore dress
blooming red—

Woozy in the back of my
soon-to-be stepdad's Volvo,
a wad of cotton wool held to
my Shirley Temple,

my mother's voice high
above my head:
the streets raced by
to Treliske Hospital
till the skylid shut.

When they removed
the stitches, I asked to keep
them, the start of an obsession
to display the things
that pained

me. I would look
at the long, black thread
legs, stiff as mother-of-the-bride
mascara: clumped lashes a-flutter
in a plastic pot.

Sylvia

The tantrumming Atlantic,
bickering gulls. A curse of drivers
on the sharp turn in, the engine's chord
change. Her 3am damson-wine

laugh, ruby with gossip. The gate
embraces us, backdoor
visitors. A sea-dripping tideline of pets
and grandchildren, body-surfing up

and down the wave hill. 'I don't know what
to cook you' quiche. A dance of china
dolls behind glass. The hand-pat of earth
as she styled her roses. Waltzes, foxtrots,

songs from *Mamma Mia*. My latest
boyfriend met with cooed approval
– *such nice hands, ate all his food.*

A panic of birds after the solar eclipse.
The flash-circle of cameras
arcing cliff to cliff, our Perranporth view.

When the text alert sounds—
my mother, telegramming death
in a roomful of strangers—
I see the Bosphorus,
but hear the Atlantic.

The Elephant Fayre

You were in a hurry to leave
home. The summer of '85, and you were
six. At Port Eliot you struck out

alone. Across the fields,
under the cover
of long grass, wild flowers, you raced
flutterbies. Certain you belonged
at this festival of gadabouts,

you listened to the breeze,
heard your calling, found
a new family— a gypsy
caravan to call

your own. They paid you
in ice cream, then – the traitors –
they gave you back.

Prep

1. Packing
You've tucked your 30-year-loved trunk into
a corner, cohabiting
with the sofa bed that won't fit
upstairs. Like when you were first installed
at boarding school. A klutzy kid in blazer-ed dress up,
with a slick too-big briefcase, the wrong socks – breaking
uniform rules before you'd even learnt

what rebellion meant. Wine-coloured, brass-tacked,
back then the trunk puff-chested a term's worth of bedded
un-belonging. Later, it waited
long months in cellars, lofts
leaking, and garages, an art gallery, a nursery
polytunnel, empty houses almost

decorated. How flatmates scorned it, sailing
its elephantine hull down three flights
across Swansea Bay to your first-floor room.
In the salt air it swelled, turned
rust, locked shut. Your trunk says it has moved
enough, claiming wrecking age, but you coax it open.

2. Rationing
You coax it because you relished its tuck-box treats
on starved dormitory nights
after 80s veggie meals – boiled eggs stiff
in cheese sauce – pushed around
a prep-school dinner plate, almost daily. You survived
on jam and bread, rationed sweets, the joyous stodge
of jacketed potatoes. You wasted, yet ate all you could:

the thrill of Saturday movies in the boy's halls, the gift
of changing the gears on the minibus drive
back. You nearly choked each time, clean
remaking your bed: you could not match
up floral duvet corners, lumps
everywhere. You swallowed down Sundays, writing letters
home with bird bones. Fasting for morsel visits.

Thirst

My head is under
the surface,
my grandfather's hand

holding it down for 1, 2, 3,
a punishment for something,
in the flooding shallows

of the stream. The Minack sea
makes a spectacle of me, pulls
limbs deep beneath the sand

in the flash of a riptide.
Spits me out grainy,
briny-eyed, starfish-limbed.

Now I sleep beside a tumbler,
liquid lapping the brim.

Gryphaea

Fossil hunting, he found an oyster:
its Jurassic calcite curve

obscene in his hand. She thought
of the toenails of all the men she'd known:

those whose yellowing claws
were more Devil

than him. She recalled a toe-sucker who didn't last
long. Didn't want to put that

in her mouth. He only asked her
to stow it away. Gryphaea: thought to prevent

rheumatism. She knew, and clambering boulders,
bore it for him, the ache of bones.

And, in the Aftermath,

I find you, building
flat-pack furniture, me drinking
green tea. My pill-pale face wet, awake
sudden and too early, feeling sick.

You ask me to apply pressure
to joints as hands screw, drill.
I kneel before you, cushioned

from the banana

                                        slip

of the night before.

Delivery

When she collects,
spilling news
of her purchase –

a changing mat –
I realise she's pregnant. Not
fat, our Kiwi at no. 23.

The opposite of what
people say about me, blooming
with my desk job diet.

See the baby-grows
in rank: empty soldiers
on the washing line out back.

Baby Shower

Deflated,
　we plead for more bounce
　　in our balloons.

　　　This morning we are all a-sag in Asda.
　　　　A hangover of hens
　　　　　we helium our squeak back
　　　　　　with parched tongues.

　　　　　Odd-one-out,
　　　　　　her bump buoyantly up front,
　　　　　　Lucy's asking for gas
　　　　　　a few months too early.

　　　　　The cashier delivers,
　　　　　　express pumping
　　　　　　into eager rubber pouts
　　　　　at the help desk.

　　　　Fist-punch balloons bursting forth
　　　with the expectancy
of arrival.

Comet Love

He's teaching me
how to catch
a comet by its tail, how
to distinguish planes
from planets, to avoid
being drowned

in cosmic snow. He talks
of harpooning it,
piggybacking dust trails
through space, falling
feet first. He tells me

he needs to calibrate
where I'll be one decade
to the next. As he maps

my orbit I ask him
where *he'll* be
in 10 years time.

The moment lags, hiccups
in transmission, lost
satellite, a hide & seek

probe, that he answers
with the question
I asked first.

Dreckly

From 'Alright, my lover!' to
Liebling, Cariad, my patchwork
accent meets your second

language. Theatre English, grammar-
perfect. Here, we stitch our tongues
together, words flocking

like tourists across the Tamar,
the Severn Bridge in high
summer. Anglo-German a-*cwtch*,

but there are tolls to pay.

The Valley of the Butterflies

is a come-to-bed lie in a land
        of must-see myths. Instead of wings
a hibernation
        of moths shadow-blanket trees;
            a subfuse lichen sleepover.

Bus-loads of bemused tourists
        trail-traipse in church silence, seeking
HDR-worthy idol shots until trigger-happy
        phone fingers disturb,   send one

                    hurtling, a flying wound.

FriedWald

'The open sky, the trees, the air, the rustling of the leaves, the chirping of the birds: many people find that comforting. Those are moments that you don't usually experience in a regular cemetery.'

– Jana Giess of FriedWald Natural Burials

Mapless, we orienteer
through a grid
of trees to your father's,

where we stand rooted
to a minute's silence.
Later, weaving

between tree graves:
your mother, brother, you
are startled birds in flight.

Until I find your heads bowed
around an iPhone, taking turns
to check your hearts still beat.

Eisblume

We wake to frost flowers blooming across the *Wintergarten* roof.
Over bread and cheese, meats for everyone except
me: horseradish, a single boiled egg each, coffee, taken black
by everyone except me, with my hotel sachet cream. They speak

too quick to translate, use animated hands. Bodies lean towards
each other, laughing. By my third trip I know too much, though
not enough to talk. I no longer see the blossom: only ice and glass,
mystery melting to shopping lists, gardening, the weather.

Torben Mows the Lawn

In his frayed orange T
he stands brash against the bland
sky, unhandles the mower.

Behind him the neighbour's cat
table-lounges. Cobweb chairs
fold beside neglected herbs.

Gulls swoop over undressed
trees, the naked washing-line.
He runs his right fingers

across his forehead, breathes,
then stoops again, machines our strip
of land, the hum subdued by

closed glass. He neatens
edges, the grass behaving for him.

Forward. Back. Forward. Back.

Until he stops,
looks up,

our eyes mapping the rented
space between us.

Prost!

Liebling, let me drink you like Riesling,
a wine as German as you are, dry
and deliciously mouthwatering,
selected for flavour

and quality. Liebling, let me breathe
your fruity aromas – lemon, pineapple – the zesty
lime finish: I'll serve you well-chilled and enjoy
either on our own, or with a variety of light
vegetable, seafood and chicken dishes.

Liebling, apparently you match
particularly well with oriental and spicy
foods, but the empty Rennie packets
bloating about the house, your person
suggest otherwise.

                         Still I'll drink you up.
Fill the cellars with your vintage,
my head with grapes and giggles.

Traction

I keep finding myself in near-
miss situations.
Take last Thursday:

stepping off
a pavement, split-second scooting
out of the path of a speeding car,

the gasp of the passenger
as we both saw
what I nearly lost. I keep

missing so many things
these days— phones, coats,
houses, trains

~~of thought~~. Walking without
looking because my eyes are caught
up with remembering the face

of you. The shifts in time as we moved
from kissing like we didn't mean it
to kissing like we did.

Picking up the Tab

I never had you down for sorcery
      just sauce
           (brown)

Now your blackened eyes
      read spell books
over breakfast

You order
      frogs' legs with
your artichokes

Notice how
      the fork kisses
your knife on an emptied plate

Better Houses

have windows, at least
three more walls. Perhaps even a roof.
Are not quite so dizzying, not quite so gaga close
to the river frisking past the doorway.

> In its fence-less yard, the motley tree light, you blow
> bubbles and I watch small versions of myself
> inside their rainbow spheres. Me,
> drinking. Me, laughing. Me, snapping

photos as a man-chased puppy invades, hoping
for more than liquid, crashing our picnic
of crushed ice, birthday margaritas. Asking
> 'Is this your spot?'

> It is now.

> I watch myself float
> away. Watch myself burst.
Watch myself stay.

Yolk / White

I hold the keys to many houses, but
the walls of this one feel brashly
naked. This sex-starved place.

Though the letting agent tried
to sort out our commitment,
our incompatibility is shelved,
the fridge going the way of student houses:
pizza boxes,
beer cans,
curdling milks.

The radishes have gone
to seed, there is no
loo roll or toothpaste, spiders
are everywhere, and the grass

is dead. The estate agent posts
written requests to air the space between
us before public viewings.

Sends handymen / builders / decorators in
to cover over our cracks.

I clean the stains of parties and parting
from threshold to hearth to attic to gate.

Gentrifying the Area

In three short months
our streets are on
the up, like the house prices,
crowds forming on corners to bid
for tumbledown terraces at auction.

Thank us
with our strawberries and herb
garden, our five runners,
beany social climbers
racing each other up bamboo
to blue-sky investments,
blue-sky returns.

In the shed, bottles are popping
themselves in celebration.
A home is brewing,
providing baths for slugs, snails hungry
for courgettes, but easily
distracted,

and it *is* hot...
who wouldn't want a hoppy dip,
a nice golden ale
to refresh in the heatwave?

There are worse ways to be going, going
gone.

Gifts Like Honey

I run in head-first at full
tilt my mouth a-buzz with well-earned stripes

I have so many bees to tell you
I lay them at your feet and

wait I take the bees to our front door
where they build to a dying welcome

I leap
and bat at your reaction

the dying welcome builds takes
me back to the front door

waiting I lay myself at your feet
with so many bees to tell you

stripes earned and mouth a-buzz
I tilt run in head-first

Sick Cat

has lost his voice, his appetite, his desire
to climb anything. He hides, shadowy
under the bed. We think: perhaps
Sick Cat is a good cat to have; he lets us lie
in, has stopped knocking
knick-knacks off the top shelf.

We feel: guilty. Still-Sick Cat makes us
sad: at the vets I am handed a box
of tissues. On Saint Dwynwen's Day
we ask the vet to mend our breaking
hearts (and Sick Cat).

Sick Cat gets well, wakes us at 6am
again. For a day or three we do not complain
when we get up to feed him. He hunts
his former panther leap in bags and biscuits.
Weaves legs, bites ankles, is hungry
for everything.

Waste, Not Want

UK shops are rationing the lettuces, but that
is just the tip of the ice—
A cold snap in Italy: this is why you can't
have nice things: clean eating,
courgetti bolognese.

And the flooding, the rain in Spain,
puts paid to our want of salad days
for all seasons. Forget
your aubergines, tomatoes,
broccoli and peppers.

Yoga mums fight over triple-price
spinach. Market traders
have never known nothing like it,
plenty of Welsh parsnips,
potatoes and carrots.

With all that foreign produce,
it's like putting all your sliced bread
in one basket or cutting
mustard in a teacup. Don't
you start; beating a burnt bridge.

Hedgerow Cocktails

i.

Gunshots fire at 4am,
or did something
fall? A glass dropped, thrown?
Then silence.
In the morning, making coffee,
the casualty is discovered:
our last bottle of cordial.

Delicate elderflowers, foraged
in summer, bringing light
to a new home, fragrance to a fizz
of hedgerow cocktails.
Now it lacquers surfaces,
floor with a syrupy tongue,
a danger of shards.

ii.

Nine days before eviction,
our community now gated,
even the tap water turns
toxic. Local residents grenade,
ignite, set targets
ablaze. We hold hands at
the epicentre, count up

destructive (de)vices,
prepare to test our
burning potential. Knives
and forks fuse. All are
condemned as
buildings detonate, hearts
demolish us.

She Needed to Make Room

The seller was wing-
broken. Her son had flown the nest, daughter
and granddaughter returning to roost.

We only had to edge it around the corner,
this blue Gumtree sofa, but she asked
if I should, if I ought to be lifting anything,
offered a husband

on loan. Outside the wedded watched us
move, men leapt from cars and doorways with
their hands itching to prove brawn.

We refused, politely shook heads while the sofa
did wheelies on pavements, fell
off its trolley and stopped

traffic. Once through the door, remember
how I stood beneath the load,
trusting you,
as the sofa wedged itself

between us. How I felt the weightlessness
of loving.
The gravity of lasting.

The Bed Testers

Before breaking one,
we had hoped to make
this a career.

Post-coital thoughts acrobatic:
our entwined bodies bouncing
together, apart, in the hunt
for again, again,

again. Two years in and I am sprawled
across a mattress in IKEA
testing springs in electric
daylight, saying 'Remember

when...?' We look at foam
and latex, check comfort against
budget, pretend to understand

the differences. We trolley our new buy
home, rolled up so impossibly small.
We wonder at how all
of that can be contained

within. We release it from
its straps, wait for
the magic. It crackles, then bursts
to life with such delight.

We make love as if
it's our duty, fresh as that
first day, consider becoming
bed testers again.

Feathers

Saturdays, he likes to watch
the birds, focusing
his zoom lens on their bawdry.

From his hide-away
he flashes, snaps, flashes
as great crested grebes,

cormorants, herons
and coots launch
their aqua-show displays.

I find myself diving in
Cosmeston Lake
all flail and feathers,
hoping he'll take me.

From Sex Change Disco

v.

The girls are in their underwear in the Taff, shrieking
about cold nipples, river-swimming, screaming:
'Is anyone else noticing this?' But only I

can hear them as they tip and slip and wet
slick-streak inelegant against the current.

A shirtless, capped boy swaggers by our secret
beach, pulling a glowing inflatable dinghy. We've nabbed
his spot. He slings a 'you've got the right idea' our way:

our music and picnic blanket, our drinks and dancing,
a bashful Jack-the-lad smirk turns Jane.
She carries on, the boat trailing like smoke behind her.

It is sweltering. Our skin damp with sweat.
I keep dipping my feet in the water to cool:
I'm swan, laying belly to riverbed,
to wet stone, wriggling

in the hour between the dog and the wolf.

vi.

All the creatures of the dark visit to take a look
at her. She is illuminated – a city species – in a glowing

glass box. See her dance. See her flap

about. She is a moth trapped, hidden amongst the trees
and night. She is banging against the walls.

>Banging. {Banging.}
>Against the bulb. The glass.

They press their thoraxes closer, antennae alert.
They point out her strange colourings.

They ask 'boy or girl?'
We might have to dissect her to tell.

I am not there

hammering fist to your door
at 3,4,5 am. Not outside our tent
at Bestival, pissing in unison. Not tripping

over grass, not breaking things, not
broken because I saw you
kissing, again, kissing someone else. Again.

In your Facebook-leaked wedding
photo you do not look gaunt, the tie
is not bad, the suit is not sharp

as blades. My mother did not tell me never
to run off with men with curls and charm. You
did not insist I could not leave you. Did not

tantrum when I refused to let you in
to the portaloo. Did not ask me to
marry you, marry you, marry you,
though I was too nice, too nice,

too nice for you. Did not panic
when I said 'yes'.

The Phobia Memory of DNA

We inherit our fears: words twisted
in the double helix. What have you

passed on? If it is fear
of curly-haired men, cheshire-smiled

charmers, I have failed. Yet we share
an aversion to the 8-legged.

If it is knowing how to rock
little deaths, I have learnt

in echoes. I will my cells to hear
ancestral calls: gypsy blood still tells me

not to wash underwear in kitchen sinks,
and, like you, I always know

which possessions to save
from a fire. Though I scatter

them through my rooms now, stalling,
hoping to trip before I flee.

White Witch

'They'll both be famous,'
your Great Granny told you, looking
at our beached-blond heads.

At the time you thought one would
be a star on the stage;
the other could be an axe murderer.

We are still waiting
to see if your guesses –
which was which – come true.

My Brother as Firestarter

I should say thanks
to you and your faulty TV –
all my teenage poems burnt
in that fire. I would have

burned too. Everything flared
in that house: the gas hob, trousers,
candles, fights. Your temper,
worst. Things, people took flight
down the stairs. Mum

was away; you were elsewhere.
I got up with the alarm, ironed
my white and black waitress uniform,
silver serviced my teeth, watching
Princess Diana's

funeral procession. You even
defaced all that was left
of our father. His signature
on my birth certificate,
just so you could buy fags
and other things that burn.

Pub Crawl Date

Pint one
    Rushing
Pint two
    Blushing
Pint three
    Charming
Pint four
    Gushing
Pint five
    Snogging
Pint six
    Chucking

                Out time

Pint seven
    Bawling
Pint eight
    Crawling
Pint nine
    You'll be fucking

                    lucky

On a Promise

He gives me red knickers
in the bar, brand
new. Label still stuck
to the graceless gusset.
They weren't meant
for me; at first, he shrugs:
'It didn't work out.'
I take them anyway, and
I'm laughing brassily
until
I realise
I'll wear them – her lace
knickers –
for him.

Rose-tinted

The strawberry milkshake was not to his taste.
It lacked consistency. He didn't like the feel
of sand between his toes. They parted company
like the beach and the morning tide. Later it seemed

appropriate sat on a rocky shore. She looked through
the shallows of her rose-tinted glass. A curving city
cast pretty. She gulped down another blush of bubbles
in time to wolf whistles from fermenting apples.

A bikini-clad Glastonbury tan swayed, vole-blind,
out of waters her puppy had fled from, scooting across
unsteady ground. On the slipway the waves licked
at an abandoned wheelchair, the owner bobbed

in the shallows, crutches held aloft, like swords.
The sun dropped, a lowered expectation. She covered skin
now curdling to raspberry ripple.
Shook stones from her shoes.

The Art of War

i.
I once asked what he wanted from me
and he said: I want you waiting,

ii.
naked on this tiled floor. I want you waiting,
winter-chilled and idle in the expectation of me,

I want you prone to submission.
I want you, waiting, waiting here for me.

iii.
How long for? I ask. Dressed
at my desk. Already bored, sharpening

pencils, I separate paperclips, bin
notes, dictate instructions.

iv.
Until I'm ready, he replies.

v.
He scatters coins, loose change, across
        the counter, casts a 'Well you won't starve,
                will you?' over his shoulder as he leaves.
vi.
I wait for him while he pretends
        a trip home, wait for the artillery fire

of texts. Undress his salad lies
        and silences on bottled Christmas spirit, anxiety.

vii.

Borrowing his laptop for work, the search
    box explodes engagement rings.

viii.

One, a recent bookmark, saved
    to another girl's name. An Emerald too.

ix.

I find her photo.

x.

I try out field positions, consider distance, dangers,
    whether they use the barrier method. I hide her inside

xi.

his paperback copy; return it to the same place
    on his shelf.

xii.

I plot tactics, military strategy, information
    managing, manoeuvres.

xiii.

Deleting my browsing history, I gather
    the weapon of myself.

POSTCARD TO SEATTLE

If you asked, I would tell that this is what summer used to be like. I wear shades, my hair up. Legs, feet, arms, back bare. The sand is warm beneath me. Dry. The breeze, filtered by the dunes' long grass, carries the sounds of the shoreline. Shrieks of distant teens play fighting. The rattle of keys and quickened breath of a lone jogger. A whoosh of traffic. Birds. Sea. Chatter. A hiss of BBQ'd flesh. Children's awkward hot-coal movements over shell-strewn land. The collectors, the foragers of the tideline. The squawks of greedy gulls. A man in shorts, topless, paddles at the water's edge. A dog races up to me, sniffs hello, runs off. Cute. For a dog. Small. Neat. A harried owner hurries after her shouting: 'Ruby'. Tennis ball and lead in hand. The man is wading now, waist deep, backwards. He is the only swimmer in the bay, diving under, a kick of legs, he breaststrokes. He is sunburnt. I wonder if he realises. Continuous sunshine. Families on day trips. Beaches and parks overpopulated. A lone plane cuts a cocaine line across sky blue. The Cork ferry is back. Honks three times. Grey smoke billowing. It leaves the bay with the tide. Devon seems closer. Ireland too. The bay is a glassy lake, a deep teal. The moon: in profile. Another plane in view now, a finer line. Air travel is back. The volcanic ash tantrums a little less these days but still cancels flights. People holiday like the 70s. Head to Butlins and find All Yesterday's Party-going Rockers bleary-eyed, heading home where shells wash up in piles. In the distance I notice a wind farm for the first time, dancing in synchronised sequence, helicopter arms. A deserter that stands in the docklands, pulling shapes alone.

Landmark 1992

At the end of Splott's hump
every day is a Holiday
Inn. Rumours tell of island residents
dropping to their knees
in the mouth of Ocean Way
while the sun-faded watch
day turn night
turn day.

The dwellers of the Magic
Roundabout are gathering—

The taxi drivers who rant
about two tramps, the litter, the artless
'waste of public cash',
'time for a change',
'age has been unkind'.

People posted in
oversized shape-sorters—
the makeshift bed, empty cans.

A landmark,
a beacon home.

Landmark 2015. Landmark 2016.
Now, the lone prostitute
snarl-pouts in pastels
trick-turning, charms Guttersnakes
in Golf GTIs to crawl past her
grassy verge to Keen Street.

Notice her new trainers,
see how she moons the sky.

The girl who claims she lived there
her moods flashing traffic light warnings,
like flares for ships lost in the night—
A pyramid of sign confusion,
she was going nowhere and everywhere at once.
Still, it's a monument

to something. Despite all the arrows,
the metropolitan hieroglyphs,
cars find their way. But she's
still lost,
where spotlights flash,
    round and round and round—

Test Card

Now see this
picture of a girl
with a clown and remember

what it means
for a channel to be
off air. Breathe

in. Breathe out. Scroll down
the stairwell, and please click
'exit'. Assemble yourself.

Up the stairs, the accounts
team are inhaling smoke
for the first

and last time. Do not
stay statue-still
with conducting
hands, those fidget thumbs.

In case of fire
exit building
before tweeting.

Inside You

You pause for breath at each front door. You press
hard. You wait for your self

to open up, to let you in with secrets.
You knock and silence breeds tinnitus

pain in your ears. You head home but have forgotten
your keys. You will the kitten to help. This time

you don't knock, instead giving in to local customs:
phoning your own mobile, hollering your own name

from the other side of the street. Inside You berates
Outside You for not ringing the bell like a decent human being.

Notes

Gryphaea: a fossil more commonly known as Devil's Toenail.

Dreckly: colloquial Cornish for the Welsh 'I'll be there now in a minute', but less hopeful.

The Valley of the Butterflies is a site on Rhodes, Greece that is visited each summer, not by butterflies, but by red-winged tiger moths.

Sick Cat: Saint Dwynwen is the Welsh patron saint of lovers and sick animals. She is celebrated throughout Wales on 25 January.

The Art of War is an ancient Chinese military treatise attributed to the military strategist Sun Tzu. The text is composed of thirteen chapters, each of which is devoted to one aspect of warfare and it is commonly thought of as a definitive work on military strategy and tactics.

Acknowledgements

An earlier version of 'Yolk / White' was published in *The Lampeter Review*.

The 'Sex Change Disco' poems are from a longer sequence of writing created for a collaborative performance with the artist Beth Greenhalgh. A Made in Roath commission, these were performed in a disused pet shop for the Cardiff festival in 2016 and then further developed to perform as part of The Garden of Earthly Delights at Cardiff Contemporary later that year. The pieces were written during my artist-in-residence at The Mothership, Dorset.

An earlier version of 'Pub Crawl Date' appeared in *Square Magazine*.

An earlier version of 'On a Promise' appeared in *The Antagonist*.

An earlier version of 'POSTCARD TO SEATTLE' appeared in *Leaf Writers' Magazine*.

An earlier version of 'Test Card' was an Ink Sweat & Tears Pick of the Month.

'A Beginner's Guide to Mourning', 'Sylvia', 'Dreckly' and 'Torben Mows the Lawn' all began to take shape at the Autumn Poetry Masterclass 2016 at Ty Newydd.

I thank you, and you, and you…

Thanks to Zoë Brigley for her skilled editing, kindnesses and friendship, for allowing me to disrupt her summer holidays, for her thoughtful suggestions, for pushing me harder.

Thanks to Richard Davies and Gillian Griffiths at Parthian, for letting me publish this book even though they'd prefer me to finish a best-selling novel. Thanks also to the rest of the team for all the behind the scenes work.

Thanks to Ty Newydd, Literature Wales, Gillian Clarke and Imtiaz Dharker for my place on the Autumn Poetry Masterclass 2016. We'll always have *Cynefin*, dears.

Thanks, fizz and nibbles to the delightful poets I share Inksplott and Answers on a Postcard workshop afternoons and evenings with: Emily Blewitt, Mark Blayney, Zillah Bowes, Rhian Edwards, Julie Griffiths, Rebecca Parfitt, clare e. potter, Kate North, Amanda Rackstraw, Tracey Rhys, Katherine Stansfield, Christina Thatcher and Hilary Watson.

Thanks to Anna and The Mothership, Dorset for the time to write, to garden and to be alone.

Thanks to all the hosts and open mic nights where I cut my performance teeth and made good friends including Amy Wack and Leona Carpenter (First Thursday), Meinir Min Evans and Seimon Pugh-Jones at Tin Shed, Laugharne, Dominic Williams and the late Anthony 'Trance' Jones (Poems & Pints, Carmarthen), Mab Jones and Ivy Alvarez (numerous), Adam Sillman and Graham Isaac (The Crunch) and really, just too many to list here, you know who you are.

Thanks to Lucy Llewellyn, Tomos Owen, Nick Fisk, Tim Wells, Chrissy Williams and Jo Bell for publishing some of my first poems. Thanks to all at Dylans Mobile Bookstore and Geoff at 5 Cwmdonkin Drive for various literary adventures and rescues.

Thanks to my friends, especially Helen Finney, Jonathan Powell, Beth Greenhalgh, John Abell, Julia Jay, Carole Burns, Penny Thomas, Sophie McKeand, Natalie Ann Holborow, MAO Oliver-Semenov, Bethany Pope, Gareth Writer-Davies, Tyler Keevil, Jonathan Anderson, Jen Abell and Dave Oprava (and those already mentioned) for regularly reminding me to write and not only edit others and for the terrible first drafts some of you read along the way.

A mouthful of bee thanks to Hooper, my witch cat, for the company, the harsh criticism and fur-warmed feet.

But most of all: *vielen Dank* Torben Schacht, *Cariad*, for this book's stylish jacket, for the keys to your Riverside flat that let me move myself in, shrink your walls and then move us both out… and everything good since. I didn't know how much better things could be, until you.

Oh, and thanks to you, fuming that I forgot your name, or decided not to include it. This isn't The Oscars BUT I thank you too.